TOOLS FOR TEACHERS

- **ATOS:** 0.7
- **GRL:** B
- **WORD COUNT:** 34

- **CURRICULUM CONNECTIONS:** nature, rocks

Skills to Teach

- **HIGH-FREQUENCY WORDS:** a, all, at, has, is, look, the, this
- **CONTENT WORDS:** bumpy, colorful, dull, fossil, rocks, smooth, surprise
- **PUNCTUATION:** periods, exclamation points
- **WORD STUDY:** oo, pronounced as long /oo/ (*smooth*); short /oo/ (*look*); multisyllable words (*bumpy, colorful, fossil, surprise*); r-controlled vowels (*colorful, surprise*)
- **TEXT TYPE:** information report

Before Reading Activities

- Read the title and give a simple statement of the main idea.
- Have students "walk" though the book and talk about what they see in the pictures.
- Introduce new vocabulary by having students predict the first letter and locate the word in the text.
- Discuss any unfamiliar concepts that are in the text.

After Reading Activities

Rocks in the book were described as being bumpy, smooth, colorful, etc. Offer some descriptive words and have children discuss whether they might apply to rocks they've seen. Have they seen a blue rock or a pointy rock?

Tadpole Books are published by Jump!, 5357 Penn Avenue South, Minneapolis, MN 55419, www.jumplibrary.com

Copyright ©2018 Jump. International copyright reserved in all countries. No part of this book may be reproduced in any form without written permission from the publisher.

Editorial: Hundred Acre Words, LLC **Designer:** Anna Peterson

Photo Credits: iStock: GoodLifeStudio, 12–13; Wavebreakmedia, 14–15. Shutterstock: Dasha Petrenko, 6–7; Eky Studio, 2–3; Jiri Vaclavek, cover; laaisee, 4–5; lcrms, 1; Maryna Pleshkun, 10–11; olpo, 8–9; Suzi Nelson, 14–15.

Library of Congress Cataloging-in-Publication Data
Names: Mayerling, Tim, author.
Title: I see rocks / by Tim Mayerling.
Description: Minneapolis, Minnesota: Jump!, Inc., 2017. | Series: Outdoor explorer | Audience: Age 3–6. | Includes index.
Identifiers: LCCN 2017045155 (print) | LCCN 2017044083 (ebook) | ISBN 9781624967214 (ebook) | ISBN 9781620319451 (hardcover: alk. paper) | ISBN 9781620319468 (paperback: alk paper)
Subjects: LCSH: Rocks—Juvenile literature.
Classification: LCC QE432.2 (print) | LCC QE432.2 .M313 2017 (ebook) | DDC 552—dc23
LC record available at https://lccn.loc.gov/2017045155

OUTDOOR EXPLORER

I SEE ROCKS

by Tim Mayerling

TABLE OF CONTENTS

I SEE ROCKS

Look at all the rocks!

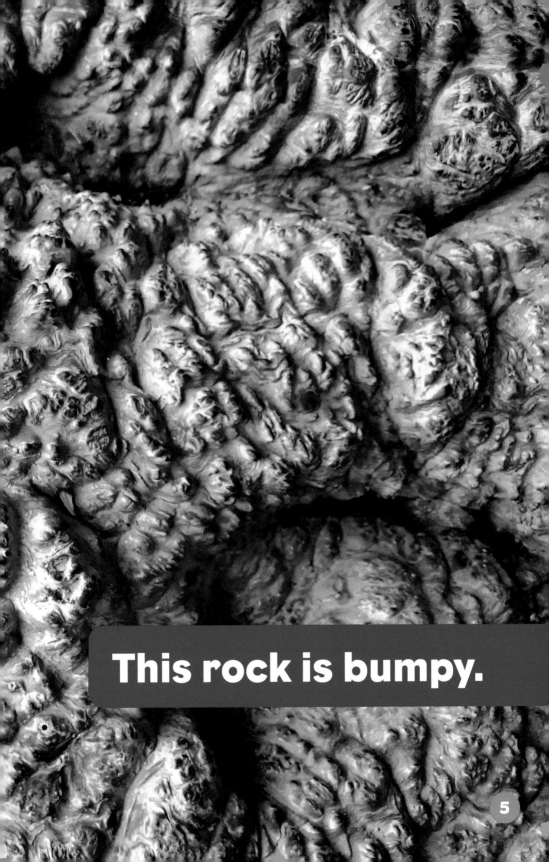

This rock is bumpy.

This rock is smooth.

This rock is colorful.

This rock is dull.

fossil

This rock is a fossil.

This rock has a surprise!

WORDS TO KNOW

bumpy

colorful

dull

fossil

rocks

smooth

INDEX